THE PREMARITAL COUNSELING GUIDE

O RANDALL JENKINS, DEdMIN

WESTBOW
PRESS®
A DIVISION OF THOMAS NELSON
& ZONDERVAN

WestBow Press books may be ordered through
booksellers or by contacting:

WestBow Press
A Division of Thomas Nelson & Zondervan
1663 Liberty Drive
Bloomington, IN 47403
www.westbowpress.com
844-714-3454

ISBN: 979-8-3850-1994-6 (sc)
ISBN: 979-8-3850-1995-3 (e)

Library of Congress Control Number: 2024904042

Print information available on the last page.

WestBow Press rev. date: 02/28/2024

CONTENTS

INTRODUCTION

Premarital counseling serves couples, families, and communities. Building a foundation for marriage takes hard work and sacrifice from the couple and those who help prepare them for the adventurous journey ahead. Both the couple and counselor must find a way to break through the quiet and superficial to engage in conversations of the heart. Things that matter the most. Therefore, the couple and counselor share the responsibility of assuring the investment of time is productive in building a foundation of trust ready for building a lifelong relationship.

You as a counselor, life coach, or consultant have invested time and energy in building a storehouse of knowledge and resources to better serve others through the use of best practices. This premarital counseling guide compiles best practices from numerous sources you know and trust, some timeless principles as well. Additional space is included for your notes and insight. Exposing each couple to wise counsel from a variety of complementing sources highlights the importance of supporting agencies, whether state or church sponsored, who agree preparing for marriage builds a foundation for a truly successful marriage and stronger family unit.

The Florida Constitution contains elements of faith and most legal documents in local or county agencies include the importance of spiritual counsel to couples and families. Because the State, Church, and most faith organizations desire successful marriages, some terminology and phrases carry similar meaning. Counselors with a faith foundation will readily recognize biblical parallels and doctrine and adapt conversation to such. Not every state has the same regulations or expectations. Counselors may find encouragement once they read of their state's desire to have and support successful marriages and families.

This guide is unique to the counseling and ministry profession, combining best practices that speak to the success of marriage. Secular, religious, and cultural issues rarely change the primary motivation for marrying, love. This premarital counseling guide is a resource for biblical doctrine while allowing ministers in all denominations to have confidence in its relevance to all marriages without being critical of church traditions.

Each topic discussion includes four characteristics of love compelling a couple to marry: heart, soul, mind, and strength. Heart, soul, mind, and strength are defined within the context and counseling practice of

TwoTwentyfive Inc., a faith-based ministry for couples, families, and communities of faith. The priority of TwoTwentyfive is providing resources and partnering with couples, families, communities of faith, churches, counselors, and pro-family groups to build strong and successful families and marriages who provide a positive impact on others. TwoTwentyfive adapts heart, soul, mind, and strength to love languages made popular by Gary Chapman: action, touch, time, verbal, gift. Common secular phrases: "I love you with all of my heart," "soul mates," "we think alike," and "I would do anything for her," adapt well to counseling and parallel the supreme love God requires of those who would love Him (with all of your heart, soul, mind, and strength) and to the love languages of God throughout the balance of Scripture.

CHAPTER 1

Love Defined

Prior to meeting with an engaged couple, you as a counselor must have a personal understanding and definition of love and how love is expressed within the context of relationships, especially that of marriage. Love defined from a faith perspective incorporates strongly held beliefs that each counselor will have developed through experience, academia, and personal spiritual journey. The official documents of the state of Florida include shared Judeo-Christian values and terminology while expectations are presented in a more sterile or contract-type perspective. This should not diminish the value of love when discussing why the couple would desire to marry.

Although dictionaries vary in defining love, most use similar terms: passionate affection, deep affection, strong liking, emotion of affection, strong devotion. When the terms are attached to one's faith or spiritual heritage and beliefs they are increased exponentially. This guide assumes the counselor has explored his or her personal beliefs and practice of such prior to engaging in leading couples to express their love in conversation and later within the context of marriage. The contract of love, when wrapped in marriage, becomes a lifelong act of selfless compassion and sacrifice for another's good. Therefore, before entering into conversation with an engaged couple, be sure of your personal view. Each couple is unique in their expression of love. Not all couples may agree with the counselor's personally held faith doctrinal values.

What are the requirements of love in the realm of government versus the realm of faith or secular morality? The state of Florida recognizes the impact of love rather than defines it. Marriage from the State's perspective is one of legality, providing regulatory qualifications, expectations, protections and rights for each spouse, protection for children and any assets, and guidelines for dissolution of marriage. Such language seems distant to that of defining love, yet it does imply action, planning, and commitment from each person willing to enter a marriage relationship. Those desiring marriage will enter into such a relationship with or without wise counsel. Your task as the counselor is to walk the couple through the "contract of marriage" as defined by the state while holding up the supremacy of love as they have so defined in conversation.

Love that compels a couple to enter into marriage reveals an understanding of selflessness and sacrifice that goes beyond a contract. Being united in marriage in Florida does not mean the couple agrees with the state's view of marriage. However, each couple, and counselor, should appreciate the state's concern that each couple be prepared for marriage in such a manner as to enjoy a long and prosperous marriage. Florida recommends every couple have the opportunity to seek counsel from their spiritual or faith leader, or qualified credentialed marriage counselor. Each couple chooses how to define and express their love as they grow among family, friends, and community. This is their life's legacy among family, friends, and community.

Including the heart, soul, mind, and strength in conversation requires commitment to the counseling process. The terms have unique connections to the love languages. The conversation guide addresses the terms as follows: Heart is the passion and intimacy longed for and pursued, Soul implies the connection of "forever-and-always-mine" commitment of each couple, Mind unites the couple's thoughts, dreams, and knowledge, Strength includes all of the resources available to the couple whether physical or otherwise. Examples are given in each section.

Chapter 2

———⚭———

Heart, Soul, Mind, Strength

Each counselor and minister define heart, soul, mind, and strength within the context of their calling, practice, and faith values. Although academia may offer broad terms applicable to general counseling and understanding, personal experience refines those terms within the context of practice. Counselors adhere to the doctrine, statement of faith, or standard operating procedures of the agency they represent. The following definitions reflect TwoTwentyfive's ministry, including terms familiar in counseling traditions, official statutes, state regulations, as well as basic morality standards most state constitutions recognize.

The heart is the center of emotion. Mankind's desire to understand the complexity and extremes of our emotions may never be satisfied. Expressed within the context of marriage, love unites two emotional beings into a powerful force. This force multiplies the passion each feels and expresses, both positive and negative. Positive emotions can strengthen or empower the couple through even the most difficult circumstances. However, if not held in check, negative emotions have the capacity to destroy.

The heart is sensitive, affectionate, compassionate, and responsive. It influences how the body and mind respond to stimuli. The heart contains man's passion, sensitivity, fears, and affections. Positive emotions such as love, joy, inspiration, awe, peace, humility, hope, excitement, pride, patience, kindness, goodness, etc., benefit the marriage relationship. Negative emotions such as fear, dread, anxiousness, doubt, shame, helplessness, anger, etc., are harmful. Couples must not fear negative emotions, rather, they must resolve to overcome them with love. Develop your best definition of heart as you interview couples, invest in the lives of your community, and fellowship with your peers. A wholly complete man or woman enjoys an emotionally healthy heart. "With all of my heart" includes everything the emotional being is capable of expressing. Couples with a healthy heart do not fear expressing their emotions.

The soul of man has eternal value. The soul contains the purpose and will of the individual. If the soul describes one's purpose, will, and being, it is the spirit that brings the soul to life, igniting and inspiring the mind, heart, and body. The soul allows us to recognize life itself, realizing the sanctity of life and vulnerability. The spirit within the soul motivates the whole being to act upon that life: expressing emotion, being creative, working, moving, sustaining, and multiplying. Couples believing themselves to be "soul mates," recognize they have compatible purposes and wills. They are not opposites; they complement and complete one another. The couple becomes each other's best friend, coach, cheerleader, teacher, partner, and lover.

The mind includes man's thoughts and reasoning, organizing man's thoughts, desire, understanding and emotion. Conscience and unconscious thought are a part of the mind. Forgetfulness, thoughtlessness, concern, importance, all affect the marriage as the couple grows together. Marriage assumes the attentiveness of the mind and being fully engaged to respond to the other's need. The mind continues to evaluate and set standards and expectations. Couples continue to develop reasoning and understanding through years of experience, building memories and wisdom to last through difficult seasons of life, especially the later years of life.

Strength includes all resources, assets, and liabilities: finances, skills, talents, fitness, property, education, status, authority, etc. Strength is gained or lost related to its use or interest. Whatever strengthens the marriage relationship and family is monitored or adjusted to produce the best results. Husbands and wives giving all they have to the marriage invest all of their strength. Marriage and family require funding for essentials. Investing one's best effort and strength early allows security in times strength has been lost through age, illness, relocation, or reduction in assets. When physical strength wanes, couples must rely upon other sources of strength that have been set aside for that purpose.

CHAPTER 3

The Six

What makes a successful marriage? What common characteristics are present in successful loving marriages? Every couple will have differing experiences. Unlocking the couple's understanding or acknowledgement of a topic builds a foundation of knowledge that can be accessed in seasons to come. The following are six of the most often cited topics found most beneficial to a happy and successful marriage. The topics were gleaned from surveys, counselors, ministers, and resources compiled in the Marriage Resource for Counselors at the conclusion of The Premarital Counseling Guide.

The counselor's challenge is to know the best available resources to recommend or review for couples and peers while acknowledging some resources are simply timeless: faith traditions, legacy couples who share their experience and wisdom, basic financial principles, and local and state laws. A compassionate counselor improves his or her own skills through investing in the interview process. This requires taking notes, understanding the couple's goals, customizing the topics in order of importance to their marriage, and time. The following topics are offered as a starting point and meant to be adapted as the interview proceeds.

Commitment

The state of Florida has communicated its interest in supporting and encouraging couples to have a long lasting, happy, and healthy marriage. As such, the Florida bar developed a handbook that highlights several key characteristics of a marriage that is prepared for each season of marriage. Beginning with premarital counseling, the state of Florida recommends every couple seek wise counsel as they start out their journey together and navigate the years ahead. Wholehearted commitment is important to the integrity of the marriage relationship.

Of the four "main items to consider" prior to marriage, commitment to one another remains at the top of the list. Counselors representing faith and religious agencies agree. The commitment of husband and wife strengthens their love for one another as they grow together in the years to come. Understanding the spiritual nature of commitment from the couple's faith tradition moves the conversation from a simple agreement of "I do" to the stronger resolve of "'til death do us part." A marriage without the foundation of commitment begins ill-prepared.

Secular and faith agencies agree. Of the surveys and resources reviewed, commitment continued to be one of the top concerns of couples. As you, the counselor, navigate through the following questions, seek to strengthen the couple's understanding of commitment, and ask them to define their expectations. Each topic includes a discussion leading the couple to define terms and resolve to grow together in knowledge and practice.

<u>Conversation with the Bride and Groom.</u>

How does the couple invest their heart, soul, mind, and strength in their commitment to one another? How do they *currently* express to one another their commitment to their marriage with each love language? How do they *plan* to continue expressing their commitment with each love language?

<u>Continued Conversation:</u>

Time: Daily, Weekly, Future planning. What priority does intimacy play in spending time together? Do each pursue the other in matters of the heart? How does each plan to fan their passion? How will the couple commit to spending time together? Spending time together allows each to share creative thoughts and inspiration. Time is a nonrenewable resource. Being present in the marriage relationship requires commitment. What is the value of time to each?

Act: Acts of Appreciation, Honor, or Recognition.

How does the couple express honor or appreciation to one another? Notes? Letters? Calls? Flowers? Opening the door? Acting as a "true gentleman" in every way? How often are each affirmed in conversation with family, friends, or peers? How much effort is required to show appreciation?

Gift: Priority to Spouse first. A loving heart is a giving heart. Expressing commitment to one another through gifts shows thoughtfulness and sacrifice. How is each appreciated more through receiving or giving gifts? What gifts show commitment the most? What is an appropriate gift to show commitment? How does each express commitment through thoughtful gifts? What priority is given to others regarding gifts that may hurt the spouse in regard to commitment?

Verbal: Affirmations, Encouragement, Challenge, Being your spouse's number one fan and cheerleader. How do you use terms of endearment to affirm love in marriage? What are shared dreams and plans as you pursue commitment? What ways to you currently show your spouse you are their number one fan?

Touch: Holding hands, Snuggles, or Simply being present to touch (nearness). Who reaches out first to hold hands or sit nearby? What arrangements have been made to assure a physical commitment to touch? How does the furniture, bed, rooms, and vehicles show a commitment to touch?

Communication

After an introduction to common values, the Family Law Handbook lists communication as a priority skill in marriage. The Handbook is a downloadable resource with valuable information that aids the couple in connecting the stern language of law to personally held beliefs from faith values, secular values, and family tradition. The state of Florida continues to advocate for strong and successful marriages by providing this handbook that complements the beliefs of most religions or faith communities.

Help each couple understand and recognize communication includes both verbal and non-verbal language. This requires each participant to have adequate time to listen and respond with understanding and compassion. Honest communication while discussing heated topics or sensitive issues will require each party to practice being patient with the other. The love language of every couple and individual is unique. Remind couples relationship skills can be learned; relationship skills can improve over time. Be patient.

Conversation with the Bride and Groom.

How does the couple invest their heart, soul, mind, and strength in honest communication with one another?

What current communication issues are a concern? How do they show one another their commitment to honest communication in their marriage? What are improvements that can be made prior to marriage? Who communicates best? Worst? What are stumbling blocks to communication?

Time: Prioritizing Communication, Making Time for Thorough Conversation, Giving Time for Responses, Patience/Waiting. How is immediacy communicated? What are some topics that hold a "cannot wait" status? What are topics that can wait? When is the best time to discuss important decisions? How long does each wait for a response? When are the best times to discuss dreams and plans for the future? How does the couple know when they have reached a decision or completed the conversation? Who decides to continue or postpone?

Act: Non-verbal Responses, Awareness, "Actions Speak Louder than Words." The heart can be crushed by non-verbal responses or actions. How does each respond or recognize the others non-verbal communication? How does the place of conversation affect the actions of the other? Intimidated? Ridiculed? Frustrated? Protected? How does touch or nearness help or hinder conversation for the couple? How soon is action required afterward? How does each coach the other in how to discuss items in a logical or rational manner?

Gift: The heart is the center of giving the gift of

communication. Love that pours from the heart will prioritize the best conversations are protected and held in a more intimate atmosphere. How does the couple use prepared dialogues to express love? What are the favorite terms of endearment they only share with one another? How does each share dreams through letters, special notes, texts, physical gifts that have special meaning, or words timed with perfection? What special lyrics, poems, or stories remind one another of their commitment and love for one another?

Verbal: While it is true "actions speak louder than words," the words we speak can fall into several categories that help or harm good communication: tone, profanity, volume, sarcasm, praise, intimidation, etc. How one speaks is as important in marriage as what is being said. How often does the couple exchange verbal affection or encouragement? When did each share a dream or intimate thought? How comfortable are they in sharing secrets with one another? How does the couple protect one another from harm as they disagree? (Conflict resolution will be covered later, but it is important to know honest communication now will soften the conflicts that may come later) Has the couple agreed to limit profanity, hurtful, and certainly abusive words? What are the plans each has for shoring up their verbal tones and language? How will they commit to giving each their best conversation?

Touch: Touch within the context of a loving marriage welcomes intimacy, boosts confidence, supports weakness, offers comfort, and enjoys spontaneity. Touch can also hurt. A heart of love and compassion will desire touch that expresses the same. A warm embrace or holding hands communicates oneness and peace. Discussing touch with a couple may bring up hurtful memories. Be prepared to help a couple work through difficult conversations. Couples who are committed to the task of preparing for marriage deserve the counselors best efforts or resources. Who most often initiates touch? How does the couple communicate what is pleasing or unwelcome? What are appropriate times and places for tough? How will touch be protected in the marriage relationship when the couple is out of the home?

Intimacy

Intimacy is a natural part of marriage: sexual, conversation, presence, or touch. The conversations and topics surrounding intimacy are necessary. Any awkwardness or anxiousness regarding being completely exposed to one another can be discussed and turned into anticipation for the journey ahead. Honest conversation about past experiences, good or bad, are needed. The counselor should not feel pressured into being a sex therapist but being prepared to ask questions and offer sound moral principles will help the couple establish a healthy view of intimacy within their marriage. Counselors with a faith or ministry background may choose to reflect on biblical principles that were established in Genesis and affirmed throughout the rest of Scripture. There are numerous Christian authors and resources available for the couple's encouragement or to answer personal questions. Several are included toward the end of the book.

Conversation with the Bride and Groom.

How does the couple invest their heart, soul, mind, and strength within the context of intimacy? (Emotions, worth and purpose, thoughts, body) How does the bride and groom plan to cultivate healthy intimacy after the honeymoon? What are the concerns prior to marriage? When did each have an appointment for a physical? (If not, it would be beneficial for each to have a physical prior to the wedding and honeymoon. Prevent surprises.) Does the couple have a plan for pursuing one another? (Some of the questions in personal health will relate to the issue of intimacy.)

Time: Prioritized, planned, anticipated, spontaneous, protected. Intimacy requires time. Has the couple planned on making sure they spend time alone? How does the couple spend their time together? Does each heart long for and pursue one another? How do they make moments of intimacy a priority? How often do they anticipate intimate moments? Who takes the lead in planning moments or being sure other events or activities do not replace intimacy?

Act: Moving toward one another with anticipation. Prior to intimacy both husband and wife come to understand what excites and builds anticipation. What acts of honor or appreciation does the wife need or want? How does each show respect or desire for the other in preparation? What simple acts of affection are shown daily? What acts are appreciated more than others? How does the couple define the difference between the act of sex and the emotion of love? How are these intertwined? (Counselors from a faith background may need to assist with defining from a biblical perspective.

As the couple ages, more emphasis begins shifting to heart, soul, and mind rather than perhaps the act of sex. More is discussed in the personal health section.)

Gift: Intimacy is exclusive to the spouse. When intimacy is compromised or not prioritized, trust and passion are lost. How are thoughtful gifts used to show intimacy? How does the couple remind one another of their love through giving? (Gifts known only to one another, song lyrics, scents, clothing, massage, oils/lotions, books/magazines, etc.)

Verbal: Affirmations, encouragement, and desire. Putting intimacy into terms that will create a reciprocal desire for closeness takes time and practice. How does the couple use words to strengthen their bonds of marriage? What do they listen to or read for more inspiration to please or encourage one another? (Counselors representing faith agencies or religious denominations should have current resources available that complement the couple's beliefs.)

Touch: Holding hands, snuggles, or simple presence to be able to touch (nearness). Intimacy can be sensual, playful, supportive, or comforting. The warmth of touch within an intimate setting brings the couple's hearts, minds, and soul closer in emotional release. Who initiates touch? How has touch drawn the couple together? How does each desire to be touched? (Some questions can be rather personal and private. These are not meant to be investigative, but rather thought-provoking questions.) What is appropriate and not appropriate? What are the thoughts of each on being coached by the other regarding what is pleasing or uncomfortable? What are boundaries when in public?

Finances

Finances are a major concern as the reason for marriage breakdowns. Unwise stewardship and debt cause undue hardship and stress. There are a number of free resources online or offered as a service of banks and other financial institutions. Employers may offer employees recommendations as well as seminars or coaching. Some counselors offer financial coaching or recommend another agency. The couple untrained in financial responsibility will lack discretion and planning for the future. Counselors counseling from a faith perspective have the benefit of numerous resources available through denominational offices and like-faith agencies.

Marriage requires funding. Homes, utilities, transportation, recreation, entertainment, communication: these all have a cost. Balancing the family budget is foundational in a couple's success. Living within their financial means takes discipline and sacrifice. Plans for the future depend on present financial practices and how the couple define success. Your task as counselor isn't to define their financial success but to prompt their consideration of what they expect and how they will accomplish the task.

<u>Conversation with the Bride and Groom</u>.

How does the couple invest their heart, soul, mind, and strength while cooperating in the goal of financial security? How do they *currently* define financial success and stewardship? What resources are they using now? Who is the most likely to overspend, save, or use a budget? Do they have or will they have joint accounts? How often do disagreements arise regarding financial decisions? What are financial resources they have used in the past that were successful? What are their concerns for now and the future? Do they keep good records?

Time: Budgets and finances require input from husband and wife. Stewardship is a skill that can be learned over time much like other life skills. How does the couple schedule time for balancing budgets and reconciling bank accounts? How often do they discuss financial planning for items outside of necessities (recreation, entertainment, gifts, etc.)?

Acts/Gifts: Acts of appreciation, honor, or recognition mostly tie in with gifts regarding finances; spouse always having first place. While balancing the family budget, couples would do well to plan on setting aside funds for special events, celebrations, spontaneous gifts of affection or endearment, date nights, etc. How often does the couple spend time with one another out of the weekly routine of work and leisure? What are small gifts that speak to their relationship and experience together? (Candies, drinks, restaurants, movies, magazines, games, trinkets, hobby items, etc.) How often do they receive or send flowers, cards, or gifts to one another at work or home? How are special milestones or anniversaries celebrated? What plans are there in place to save for personal gifts of affection?

Verbal: Affirming and encouraging one another through financial difficulties or decisions unites the couple and home into one heart and mind. Decisions and planning require honest communication. Most couples will face decisions regarding major purchases, moves, job changes, training, education expenses, overdrafts, or crisis of a sort. Honest verbal communication keeps the couple from hording funds or criticism. Who has the natural skills and interest in family budgeting? Encourage them. Who spends too freely and lacks financial discipline? Be patient, use small steps in training. Allow input for budgeting and map out a plan for spending *and* saving. Who is most verbal about staying within the budget? Communicate with one another.

Faith

The Florida Family Law Handbook recommends couples seek out a counselor, a trusted clergy member, or other available resource prior to marriage. The State does not assume every couple participates as a part of a faith community or church yet does understand the value of wise counsel from clergy members who have traditionally been a part of solemnizing the bond of marriage. Counselors from a faith tradition may use a couple's religious or faith background to reinforce their foundational understanding of the commitment and sacrifice needed for a successful marriage. Regardless of faith background or experience, each couple are encouraged to communicate freely their spiritual preferences.

The personal nature of one's faith and beliefs are to be understood as personal rather than something to be changed by the counselor. Disagreements about faith or beliefs should not hinder the counselor from offering wise counsel and coaching the couple through discussing their future plans. Honest dialogue and understanding are expected. Couples with differing faith traditions are encouraged to discuss those prior to meeting with the counselor or assigned before future sessions.

Conversation with the Bride and Groom.

How does the couple invest their heart, soul, mind, and strength in their spiritual growth and faith journey together? (Being one in heart, soul, mind, and strength) What are the faith and belief backgrounds of each? How often has the couple attended ecumenical services together? How familiar are they with each other's spiritual journey? When have they discussed future plans to participate in a faith community or church?

Time: Sharing like-faiths and beliefs unites the heart, mind, and soul unlike any emotion. Spending time with one another in a place of spiritual significance strengthens the emotional bonds of the couple and their family. How often does the couple spend time with one another in like-minded service or study regarding faith? How does each practice their faith and belief daily? What important holy days are observed or expected? When are expected times set apart for practicing their faith? (Church, worship, services, activities, retreats, ceremonies, etc.) Who is responsible for assuring time is invested in practicing the faith of the family?

Act: Religious acts are limitless. Honoring one another in marriage is an act of faith as is trust, self-discipline, and sacrifice. A loving heart continues to pursue the object of one's faith. The supremacy of love allows the couple to trust, forgive, and respect one another through life's most difficult moments or celebrate victories large and small. An act of faith allows the couple to attend events without the other or work extra hours as agreed upon. Forgiveness sought or given heals brokenness and allows the couple to grow in unity and appreciation for one another.

Verbal: Faith statements are used to build up character and emotional wellbeing. When the couple shares a similar or compatible faith or system of beliefs, they stand united in family planning, career mindedness, type of entertainment or leisure activities to participate, financial stewardship (charity involvement), education goals, and life planning (wills, insurance, etc.) How often does the couple discuss the above and the impact beliefs should have on decisions: family planning, charity involvement, education, wills, insurance, etc.? Who has been the most vocal regarding faith? How does the couple discuss differences in faith or beliefs?

Touch: How does the couple's faith reflect in how they touch or intimacy? What concerns does the couple have regarding different beliefs regarding intimacy or touch? Does the couple's faith or belief system hinder or celebrate touch and intimacy? What resources have been made available that complement their faith? What concerns does the couple have in continuing to celebrate intimacy and faith as a part of the other?

Family

Marriage begins or builds a family. The uniting of the husband and wife is the foundation of the family. As children are added, so grows the family. The internet has exponentially added to the resources available to those raising children. Recommending reliable resources to couples interested in building their family is a privilege for every counselor. The benefits of having a short list of resources available to the couple help build their confidence and knowledge. Personal experience in their own family should be discussed candidly with the understanding not everyone has grown up in a home filled with compassion and encouragement or with both parents.

When children are already present in the family the counselor acknowledges the mother or father has parenting experience. Premarital counseling creates an open dialogue where both bride and groom communicate honest feelings, dreams, and concerns regarding present and future children. The forthcoming marriage must include thoughtful consideration of the children and blended nature of the family. Legal obligations must also be discussed.

Conversation with the Bride and Groom.

How does the couple invest their heart, soul, mind, and strength as they become not only their own family but a part of one another's extended family? (Emotional connections, appreciation, understanding, position) What are the current desires of the couple for growing their family? What timelines have been discussed? What discussions have been made regarding careers, education, entertainment, assets, liabilities, and home?

Time: Family continues 24/7/365 once it begins. Although there are vacations, long weekends, or breaks, the family remains and demands attention. How often does the couple discuss family plans? How much time is currently spent each day with family? How is time with family prioritized? How many children are expected or desired? When do parents spend time with one another? With children? With extended family? If "home is where the heart is," how much time does each one feel is necessary to assure their heart truly belongs to their family?

Act/Gift: How are family members honored or recognized? How is love and appreciation expressed to each member? Who keeps the calendar and tracks memorable moments that should be remembered? What celebrations are currently observed or planned? What gifts are anticipated through the year for each member of the family? What spontaneous gifts have been the most memorable and timely? How are the characteristics of those receiving a gift included in the thought process for meaning and appreciation? How are gifts used to encourage, reward, acknowledge, or challenge each member? Who continues to teach the benefit and process of giving gifts? How has a legacy of giving been established?

Verbal: What is the language of "family?" Each family has cultural influences that impact verbal communication within the home. Language can be used to build up or tear down, to instruct or criticize, and to foster love or create bitterness. What is the verbal tone and expectation of the couple? Who decides what is appropriate or forbidden? How does the couple monitor their verbal and nonverbal communication with one another and with family? What expectations are there with family and extended family? What verbal and nonverbal prompts does the couple use to express warning, disappointment or disagreement, compassion, frustration, or pain?

Touch: The touch of compassion is able to quiet a frightened heart and soothe the pain of a bruised knee. Holding hands, snuggles, or simple presence to be able to touch (nearness) builds family unity. Couples will define what touch is appropriate for discipline, recreation, and intimacy inside the home and beyond. Couples also model appropriate touch that will pass down to the next generations. What concerns does the couple have regarding touch or its appropriateness within the family? What measures have been incorporated to assure family members understand welcome touch? What boundaries have been put in place to protect family members from unwanted touch?

Chapter 4

Additional Conversations

Conflict Resolution

Couples committing themselves to the exclusivity and permanence of marriage have a predisposition for fighting through the hard times of marriage. Couples investing in premarital counseling are better equipped to fight for their marriage as they navigate disagreements and challenges. The Florida Family Law Handbook previously mentioned recognizes the steps a couple takes before a marriage is dissolved. Remind the couple to review your State's official documents for helpful conversation and encouragement. Florida's handbook contains sobering information the couple want to know prior to marriage. It is better to enter marriage knowing the risks and rewards than have regrets years later when the family has grown to include children.

Compromise, diplomacy, pros and cons, debates,

and patience are just a few keys to resolving a myriad of issues sure to come up in marriage. Disagreements are a reality of living in a close intimate relationship. Couples aware of issues most likely to erupt in passionate arguments benefit from knowing strategies to resolve conflict. Resolving conflict can be learned with patience tempered with love.

Conversation with the Bride and Groom.

How does the couple invest their heart, soul, mind, and strength in navigating through conflicts? (Compassionate and responsive, respecting one another, valuing and protecting the marriage relationship, reasoning and understanding, utilizing and growing in conflict resolution skills) Not all disagreements devolve into conflict. Honest communication and understanding play key roles in resolving conflict before it reaches the point of causing emotional distress and anxiety. How does the couple currently resolve disagreements or conflict? What marks a satisfactory end to a conflict?

Time: Moment by moment, day by day. Marriage is a lifelong process of learning. Conversations require both parties to engage in listening, understanding, and confirming. Resolving conflict also requires time. How much time is required for settling disagreements? How much time does the couple commit to discussing topics or decisions that may cause disagreements? Do each give adequate time for replying without interruptions? How does the couple agree to a pause in an argument for a quiet time of prayer/meditation/silence?

Act: Each role in marriage deserves honor and appreciation. Both husband and wife are honored positions. Recognizing another's role, position, knowledge, or experience helps each member of the family temper their language and tone during conversation or disagreements. Remembering to "act honorable" keeps each from intimidating posturing. How does each posture themselves during disagreements?

Gift: Peace or forgiveness can take many forms. The act of forgiveness can be considered a gift, but at times a couple may want to express peace, forgiveness, or remorse in a tangible way. What gift/gifts have the couple given as peace offerings or as a sign of forgiveness? How should such gifts be received? What circumstances would a spouse consider appropriate for a gift? What experience has the couple in giving or receiving such gifts?

Verbal: Verbal language during an argument, or in resolving an argument, influences future arguments. Words can crush the heart and discourage the mind and spirit. "Fighting fair" reminds the couple of the scars that can remain after a long or bitter conflict. Rebuilding trust is hindered when rules of engagement are not followed. What rules of engagement have been put in place for the couple? What language or terms are not allowed? How does the couple refrain from vulgar or hurtful language, tones, or insults? What options are agreed upon for each to remove themselves from the heat of an argument? Who are their trusted family or friends allowed to give unbiased wise counsel? What experience does the couple have they do not want repeated?

Touch: Should the couple be near one another during a disagreement or heated exchange? During the conflict may not be the best time to hold hands or snuggle. Post resolution is a better time for such. Seeking forgiveness or offering forgiveness may be safer times to offer touch. Resources on effective communication during conflict resolution abound. Several are listed in the resource list.

Career

Both husband and wife contribute a career in the marriage. While one or both may have a job outside of the home, each one has a skill and role to play in the marriage and family. Counselors representing faith agencies understand each person has a calling to fulfill. Each possesses a giftedness and skill to perform and excel in their area of work. Counselors may utilize one of several online questionnaires to help each couple discover their area of interest and what career or job may suit them. Premarital counseling may not be career building, but it can help point couples to positions and jobs otherwise unknown.

Conversation with the Bride and Groom.

How does the couple invest their heart, soul, mind, and strength in supporting and encouraging one another's careers? Do the careers of the couple complement one another or compete for time and importance? How does each support the other's job and position? How does future children and childcare tie into each one's career? If children are present now, what plans have been discussed to meet the needs of the children? How will the couple manage future career or position advancements that may require relocation?

Time: Careers occupy time. Funds are required to maintain the supply of food, clothing, shelter, and life expenses. What concerns does the couple have about time spent away from one another or family? What priorities have been discussed about time with one another and family compared to time spent building a career or position? When are permissible times for each to work overtime or extra hours for pay? How does the couple invest their heart, soul, mind, and strength in their desire to enjoy and support one another's career or vocation?

Act: What recognition or honor is appropriate to celebrate a promotion or new position? How does the couple support or help one another in their professional fields of work? How often are couples able to enjoy lunch together in the workplace if at all? What is the best way each could support the other's career?

Verbal: How often does each offer appreciate for the other's work and effort? When possible, how do they ask for input on work projects? How frequently do they sincerely ask about one another's daily task of work? What words of encouragement do each appreciate the most? What journals or articles do each read or offer to be read so each can be familiar with terminology that will drive meaningful conversation? (Being genuinely interested in one another's work encourages each to do work that builds pride and a sense of accomplishment)

Touch: Work drains the mind, body, and spirit of energy. A gentle kiss, strong embrace, and quiet home can restore a weary body. What measures are in place to help one another relax once the workday is complete? How does each help the other relax and restore vigor for the next day? Touch works wonders. Remind each couple to discover strategies to welcome one another into their home of rest at the end of a weary day.

Friends

Life prior to marriage included relationships with other men and women. Couples bring separate and common friends into their exclusive relationship. Before making drastic changes in those relationships the couple needs to have an honest conversation about which friendships will strengthen their marriage and which may be toxic. Friends are important to growing a stronger marriage, but which friend? How many? Married friends or singles? What about the age of friends? Work friends? Confidentiality?

Nurturing friendships outside of the marriage relationship takes time and priority away from the marriage and family. Honest conversations at the beginning of the marriage allow boundaries to be put in place and qualifications for continued friendships. As the wedding date nears the conversations become more difficult. Talking about concerns early may spare everyone from hurt feelings.

<u>Conversation with the Bride and Groom.</u>

How does the couple invest their heart, soul, mind, and strength in one another as they appreciate the other's friendship relationships? How do current friendships help or hinder the couple's relationship? Who will be included in the wedding party standing with the bride and groom? How do friends view the couple's relationship? (For? Against?) Have all the necessary private friendship pasts been discussed? (If the husband or wife would dread or be embarrassed about a past indiscretion, it will be best to have those conversations now rather than after "I do." The counselor may want to assign that task for the couple to complete prior to the next session.) How do they protect their marriage relationship?

Time: Spouses are best friends. Spouse's former best friends are now second. The time invested in becoming a best friend can't be overlooked, and neither can the time needed for one heart to belong to another. How much time will be devoted to friendships outside the marriage or home? How will the couple include one another in their friendships and activities? How will each spouse alert the other when feeling neglected because of friends? When are unacceptable times friends should be included or welcome in the home?

Act: How does each spouse recognize the importance of activities with friends? (Sports, exclusive activities or events, seasonal outings, meals when the other is occupied otherwise, etc.) How are friendships helpful in strengthening the bonds of marriage? (Mentoring, retreats, conferences, etc.)

Gift: Priority belongs to the spouse. When

friendships receive the best or most thoughtful gifts a spouse can feel neglected. What extravagant gifts have you given in the past? How have you honored your spouse with such extravagance? (Gifts depend on budget and sacrifice. How does the couple place priority on one another?)

Verbal: Affirmations and encouragement should come from the spouse first, not the friend. How does each show they are their spouse's number one fan? What verbal and non-verbal language does the couple desire to hear or feel to know they are appreciated and loved?

Touch: Some activities among friends require touch. (Sports, games, seasonal activities, etc.) The couple should be encouraged to discuss proper physical boundaries to ensure friendships are above reproach. What activities would each prefer the other to refrain from in the future with others?

Vacation time

Couples need time to relax and recover from work. Getting a goodnight's sleep or sleeping late on occasion are important to being refreshed or enhancing a spirit of spontaneity. Budgeting for an extended time from home and work may not be possible early in marriage, but it can certainly be a dream. Creative planning in the early years of marriage allows the couple to spend less on travel while spending more time together.

Vacation as discussed in this session concerns recreational time away without obligation to work, family, schedules, etc. Although some careers require at least the possibility of availability for emergencies, the time spent with spouse and family are of utmost priority. Should a vacation involve extended time with a church or other non-profit organization's camp/retreat, planned moments for couples may be a condition for participation.

Conversation with the Bride and Groom.

How does the couple invest their heart, soul, mind, and strength as they plan and participate in recreational activities? Taking time away from career or work for an extended weekend or several days has the potential to refresh and fan the flames of marriage intimacy and growth. Families focus on one another and building a stronger bond between husband and wife, parent and child, or siblings. The couple will set a precedent early in their marriage if they choose to spend time together and build their own family vacation traditions.

Time: How often has the couple planned to simply pause at times during the year to vacation? (Extended weekends at home or away or several days) Who plans time away regularly for the family? What priority does recreation play in refreshing the marriage? How much time has accumulated for each regarding time off from current employment? What are dream vacations that require extended time? How are those being planned out in advance?

Act/Gift: How often are spontaneous trips planned to recognize special achievements or anniversaries? What are the best trips thus far? How would each enjoy being the focus of or reason for a trip away or home?

Verbal/Touch: Vacations exclusive to husband and wife involve verbal and non-verbal communication as well as touch. Second or third honeymoons, celebrations, anniversary trips: all are wonderful ways of reigniting romance and reaffirming vows. Counselors familiar with successful marriages understand the importance for couples to be together. The resources available to counselors regarding romance, vacations, creative get aways, and intimacy are almost limitless. Faith-based counselors have a number of resources available online. Freely share to couples.

Holidays/Travel

Unlike vacation, holidays and travel are the numerous family obligation trips that fulfill the duties of a responsible and loving member of the family. Holidays with in-laws. Special family life events such as weddings, funerals, christenings, baptisms, milestone birthdays, graduations, etc. Family reunions. Reciprocal is certainly possible too: hosting a family member or members for a day or overnight.

Couples not only marry one another; they marry into extended families. The moment they say, "I do," they become their own family as a part of each other's families, for better or worse. Having an honest conversation about parents, siblings, and extended family should have been a part of courtship and their time of engagement. Prior to the next scheduled meeting with a premarital counselor, the couple should be tasked with sharing family accounts with one another. Conversations bring out the best memories and perhaps hurtful accounts as well. Reminding the couple of conflict resolution may help them get through difficult conversations regarding forgiveness and reconciliation. Allowing past events to destroy present and future joy prevents the couple from moving forward in their own hopes and dreams.

Holidays and travel build family unity and strengthen bonds. Creating memories while being a part of extended family gatherings builds a culture of togetherness creating family traditions worth celebrating. Each couple has an opportunity to grow their own legacy. The cost of traveling with family for holidays or family events is rarely reimbursed; budget and communicate accordingly.

Conversation with the Bride and Groom.

How does the couple invest their heart, soul, mind, and strength in their marriage while honoring family or extended family? Once the couple becomes familiar with each other's family legacy and history they begin to establish boundaries and rules for proper behavior depending on the circumstance or family present. What past experiences remain a concern? What prompt does the couple use for alerting one another about an action or conversation that needs immediate attention? What family members are welcome in the home? Overnight? Who are designated drivers?

Time: Each couple marks special holidays or travel dates that rarely deviate from plans. What events are reciprocal with parents or siblings? (Weddings, events, etc.) How much time off is sufficient to fulfill the demand of family travel? If limited time off is available from an employer, how much vacation time is designated to family travel?

Act: Hosting or attending a family member's achievement/s strengthens the bonds of extended family. Recognizing milestones and special events celebrate the whole family. Couples expecting reciprocal action must be engaged in the life of the family. What events are scheduled in the year ahead? Who has the updated contact list of family members? How are family members most often greeted or recognized?

Gift: What hospitality gifts are appropriate or expected? Who has the responsibility for choosing gifts for events? How are gifts received? How are gifts balanced regarding cost, value, quantity, or quality?

Verbal: Loving families communicate that sentiment with one another, even when traveling or visiting one another. How does each temper conversations with loved ones to promote unity or understanding? What nonverbal cues do couples look for when discussing sensitive or intimate topics? How has the couple informed one another regarding conversations or topics to avoid? How does the couple encourage other family members to be involved in conversation? What conversations are most memorable? What conversations are they most looking forward to?

Touch: Huggers or non-huggers? Touch is simply a part of being attached to family. How does the couple manage family members who enjoy being close and those who are content with a handshake or verbal greeting? What are boundaries set among age groups or adults? When visiting overnight, what accommodations are necessary for the couple or children? What are memorable moments the couple has experienced with family? (Games, outdoor sports, accidents, etc.).

Community Involvement

The health of the home and family impacts the health of the community. A healthy marriage relationship engaged in community events or business influences other marriages and families. Counselors from a faith background have an opportunity to remind couples of the many biblical principles guiding them to represent their faith in their spheres of influence and beyond. Being confident in navigating relationships in business, recreation, community events, non-profit organizations, government involvement, or social settings allows the couple to be a positive influence.

Community involvement is not required but is encouraged. As the family grows, they will become known in certain spheres: school, church, sports leagues, associations, social or recreation clubs, business/market peers, etc. How will the couple continue to grow together while involved in their community?

Conversation with the Bride and Groom.

How does the couple engage their heart, soul, mind, and strength as a couple as they participate and become known in their community? How is the couple currently known in their community? How long have they been in the community? Who knows them outside of their marriage relationship? How does the couple want to be known?

Time: How much time will be dedicated to being a part of their community? How will the time take away from important family schedules? (Neighbors, Homeowners Associations, local teams, church, local events, etc.) What fees have been considered? What concerns are there about how much time is currently or planned dedicated to community involvement? How does the couple benefit from investing time with their community?

Act/Gift: Over time the community begins to recognize leaders and influencers. Involvement in community or organizations reveals the heart of the couple, what they are passionate about. Again, how does the couple want to be known? What skills/talents of one or both can be invested to build up the community? When asked to lead, how has the couple prepared for such discussions? How does each support the other when being honored or recognized for community involvement or awards?

Verbal: How the couple addresses one another, and others reflects personal character. Verbal and nonverbal language impacts how others view the marriage relationship and any bias to work with them on projects. Passion, knowledge, leadership, compassion, and confidence are allies of marriage. Being engaged in conversation develops friendships, builds community, and allows couples to be a part of honest dialogue. How does the couple express compassion to one another in public? What terms of endearment are most frequently used? What language is frowned upon between one another or with others? How does the couple confront inappropriate language and tone?

Touch: While in the community at home and abroad, every couple has the opportunity to enjoy public displays of affection. (Holding hands, wrapping arms around one another, hugs, a kiss, sitting near) How has the couple displayed affection? What does the couple view as an appropriate touch in public? What is not appropriate? (Each couple has freedom to express their definition of what is appropriate. However, knowledge of local ordinances or laws should not be overlooked.)

Education/Professional Training

Continuing education and professional training have become a part of America's culture. Nearly every vocation encourages some type of continued training: technology, professional services, manufacturing, military service, medical staff, science, government agencies, marketing agents, etc. Couples with one or both partners enrolled in such training make decisions based on the anticipated benefits. Understanding the reality of late nights or time away from one another builds a cooperative spirit of unity. The future implications of training or education may lead to job advancement, pay increases, relocation, or entrepreneurship. When further education or training is required from an employer the couple must discuss how household responsibilities will be shared while the requirement is fulfilled. Even so, when further education or training is voluntary, the couple should discuss shared responsibilities and shared costs.

Conversation with the Bride and Groom.

How does the couple invest their heart, soul, mind, and strength in one another and their marriage as they pursue further education or professional training?

What training or education is currently under way

or completed? If underway, when will the training be complete? What costs are involved? How will the training or education benefit the marriage and future plans?

Time: Adequate time must be given for education and professional training to be of value. This is a season for learning and acquiring new strategies for taking care of one another, meeting education goals, and budgeting needed resources. What concerns does the couple have in meeting time constraints or loneliness? How are study breaks used or time between semesters used to refresh the marriage relationship?

Act/Gift: Spousal support during the seasons of building vocational and career knowledge and skills greatly increases the sense of appreciation and sacrifice of both. Helping study or complete projects when allowed, asking questions about how to support or encourage, or providing needed activities during breaks recognizes the teamwork of marriage and preparing for the future with one another. How does the couple currently support one another through acts of support and patience during training or education? What are favored ways to support one another? What plans are in place to support one another? How has the couple been creative in supporting one another? Preparing a favorite snack or meal to celebrate accomplishments is just a small part of support.

Verbal: Regardless of skill or knowledge, each spouse can offer encouragement to one another during times of training. Challenging each other to study or complete projects, helping study, asking how to help, being a cheerleader, genuine interest, etc. Nonverbal communication helps or discourages. Helpful: eye contact, being present or available. Discouraging: walking away during conversation, crossing arms, reading, not paying attention. How does the couple verbally support or hinder? What conversations are most helpful? What are verbal prompts to communicate a desire to change the subject of school or training to something lighthearted? How are verbal and nonverbal cues used to bridge communication?

Touch: Time apart during training or meeting education goals creates a desire to reunite. When professional training or continued education conflicts with intimacy, the heart and soul may become discouraged. How does the couple maintain sufficient intimacy when training demands study or project completion? How does the couple plan to balance physical or mental intimacy with the demands of training? (Personal details remain in the confidence of the couple. Simple reminding the couple of such needs should be sufficient.)

Social Views

Couples with a firm foundation of personal values and beliefs remain faithful to those values and beliefs when social views attempt to compromise them. Technology has made it possible for couples to have access to social views that oppose or support their traditional family values. Culture wars, political correctness, personal space, entitlements, tolerance, intolerance, offensive language, profiling, and social norms are just a few terms familiar to the couple. The social views of the couple, strongly held, loosely agreed upon, indifferent, or otherwise, shape their interaction with one another, how they view or dismiss the media, and how they interact with others. Strongly held values and beliefs will help the couple maintain their character and influence while remaining confident when discussing the list of terms above.

Social media influences how couples view the culture around them and how they will interact within their community, workplace, and at times, even one another. Personal knowledge, experience, and wisdom affect how they will view the world around them. Counselors inquiring about the couple's connectivity to social media and its usage help the couples discover areas with the potential to compromise and areas needing to be safeguarded. The couple should be encouraged to define their own identity rather than succumb to what current cultural or social views repeat.

Conversation with the Bride and Groom.

How does the couple share their heart, soul, mind, and strength while participating in social action or expressing social views publicly? Social views are fluid in some areas of thought and structured in others. What major differences has the couple discussed or agreed upon? What are lingering concerns regarding differences?

Time: How does the use of social media monopolize time that could be used to discuss accurate information for helping and not hindering their relationship? When has the couple audited their use of social media? How does the couple keep media time from encroaching on meaningful conversation? What measures are in place to police time other family members spend on social media? What media outlets are limited or prohibited?

Act/Gift: Technology and media can place a spouse in a position to influence social views in an instant. How the couple responds depends upon their faith, values, and character. Assuming the attention is positive, how would the other spouse offer appreciation, honor, or recognition? What attempts have been made in the past or currently to support one another?

Verbal: How a couple responds to social views affirms their convictions both verbally and non-verbally. Speaking out or boycotting are simple means of voicing approval or disproval of a view, action, or cultural expression. How does the couple voice approval or displeasure of social views? What views do they support or have a passion for or against? How do the couple's social views support their faith and beliefs?

Touch: Social views in the marketplace are made known through what the couple consumes. (Entertainment, recreation, clothing, religious affiliation, charities, department stores, online shopping, groceries, etc.) Everything the couple consumes has social view implications. Others are influenced by their decisions, especially children and family. What social views does the couple support by what they consume? The counselor helps the couple discover how their decisions affect their social influence. Online resources from faith agencies and denominations are plentiful. Encourage the couple to audit how they consume to better support those who hold similar or complementary views.

Personal Health (Staying Healthy)

Personal health and staying healthy include the whole person: body, spirit, soul, mind. Expressing love within marriage includes physical intimacy as well as maintaining the health needed for such activity. Expressing "'til death do us part," in wedding vows implies each will maintain proper health and fitness. Total health, total fitness. Our bodies age and break down, our mind may lose the ability to remember or concentrate causing our spirit to be broken, our soul can become discouraged. Although poor physical health through neglect or illness does affect the whole person, it does not dictate a loss of strength in spirit, heart, and soul.

Maintaining a healthy lifestyle and proper diet reflects the desire each has to give wholeheartedly to being their best for one another. Grace allows the couple to grow old together as they cherish the moments and multiply their memories while appreciating their physical change as they age. There are seasons of life when intimacy abounds and seasons that seem empty. Couples aware of coming changes learn to adapt and press on through the quiet moments. Their spiritual bond of heart and mind strengthens love through life's difficult moments.

As the counselor moves through the personal health

questions, remind couples to reflect on the wholeness of their health. Body, heart, mind, and soul. What activities engage their love for one another besides that of physical intimacy? What stimulates their love and passion for one another? The medical and counseling field provides countless resources to help couples be as creative and informed as possible as they begin and continue their journey of marriage.

Conversation with the Bride and Groom.

How does the couple continue to engage their heart, soul, mind, and strength through a healthy lifestyle, setting a precedent for continued growth? (Whole-being health: heart, soul, mind, body) Heart, soul, mind, and strength are foundational truths expressed earlier. Maintaining personal health for the whole being pays huge dividends later in life. Have the couple reflect on marriages that have influenced them and the ages of those couples who continue to provide an example of loving relationships. What do they desire for their marriage? What commitments are they willing to make in pursuit of those dreams?

Time: Daily routines assist or hinder individuals in experiencing a day filled with completed tasks or failure. Does the couple incorporate prayer or quiet contemplation? How do each prepare mentally or spiritually? How is nutrition a part of their daily routine? Online resources and applications on tablets or cellphones can assist the couple in maintaining healthy habits. What is the couple doing currently to schedule time to maintain a healthy heart, soul, mind, and body?

Act: Action uses energy and burns calories. What activities do the couple share in developing and maintaining a healthy lifestyle? What treatments have been necessary to help the couple through a short term or prolonged illness? How does the couple plan to continue maintaining an active lifestyle physically, mentally, and spiritually?

Gift: Presenting one another as an exclusive gift to be enjoyed and appreciated throughout a lifetime suggests the number one priority is to one's spouse. Treating each day as a gift allows the couple to renew their passion daily and provide a "reset" when needed. Not every day goes as planned but doing their best to give to the other a life of wholehearted commitment is something to cherish. How does the couple express themselves as a gift? How does the couple enjoy daily moments? What are creative ways the couple has shown one another their love and devotion?

Verbal: Verbal affirmations and encouragement are like medicine, refreshing the heart and soul. Laughter, crying, deep emotional conversation. All of these can uplift or tear down. How does each respond to verbal appreciation and terms of endearment? What language speaks loudest to each? (Touch? Verbal? Gifts? Time? Acts of love?) Staying healthy in mind and heart requires honest and intimate conversation. What does the couple enjoy most about conversation with one another? What common topics enlighten their hearts and draw them closer?

Touch: Being physically healthy welcomes, appreciates, and attracts the other's touch. Having like-mindedness and being united in spirit attracts the other and welcomes touch. Staying healthy throughout a lifetime may not always be possible because of prolonged physical or mental illness. Couples prepare for all circumstances prior to making marriage vows. Through better and worse, sickness and health are not always manifested physically. Medical journals remind patients and loved ones the importance of touch. At times the touch of a spouse is the only thing bringing encouragement and hope, and a reminder they are cherished. What is the couple doing to prepare for the lifetime commitment of being available to touch and be touched?

Will/s

Eventually man succumbs to age or illness and passes away. While the couple enjoys the anticipation and excitement of the wedding day and honeymoon, preparing a simple will at the start of a marriage can spare each the heartache that comes through loss of life or property. Counselors able to recommend compassionate attorneys provide a service to couples who may otherwise be caught unaware of legalities they face if unprepared. Wills protect assets and family from unwelcome intrusion by government authorities or claims by those outside of the marriage relationship.

Wills allow the couple to dictate how assets or resources are allocated to best serve one another, family, foundation, or charity. Once expenses or accounts are satisfied, property is distributed as the couple has deemed most important to themselves. Wills allow the couple to designate executors who have agreed to follow their desire in distributing or investing assets. Should the couple have children, they have an opportunity to designate guardianship and establish funds that provide for the future. Creating a will is in the best interest of the couple, maintaining a current will may prove to be a blessing to heirs.

Conversation with the Bride and Groom.

How does the couple plan to invest their heart, soul, mind, and strength in the future regarding a will that benefits one another or family? Does each have a will? Have they discussed with one another or family about writing a will? Who has the original copy? What does the will include? (Home, assets, banking information, insurance policies, outstanding debts, heirs, family, medical circumstances, etc.)

Time: Now and future planning. Being concerned for one another now rather than later. How much time has the couple spent sharing their concerns for the future should a tragedy occur? What concerns do they have? What time constraints are present that prevent them from conversation?

Act/Gift: Wills recognize the desires of each person. The content of a will reflects honor and compassion to beneficiaries. Couples leave a legacy of love and affection through careful wording of wills. What life lessons or assets are important for the couple to leave behind? What are special heirlooms that they wish to remain in the family? How are assets distributed to heirs or family members as gifts of endearment or promises kept?

Verbal: Communicating desires regarding the execution of wills and last wishes may seem unnerving early in marriage. However, being candid and honest in conversation allows each to share from the heart. What are issues to discuss regarding property that should remain in the family or one of the families? How have past discussions of will and testaments ended? What resolutions remain to be discussed? Has the couple discussed video or recorded messages?

Retirement plans

Careers and vocational work eventually come to an end through necessity or retirement. Making the transition from daily work responsibilities to plans that exclude fulltime employment can be traumatic if not anticipated ahead of time. Providing the funds to meet essential needs during the season of retirement requires self-discipline and consistent adjustment to contributions. Retirement plans, information, and resources are prevalent throughout most communities. Couples have the option of consulting financial planners, employer resources, life coaches, banking institutions, and perhaps trusted and knowledgeable friends and family.

Retirement comes as a part of the marriage journey. Financial planning becomes less of a concern as a couple begins to understand the importance of their relationship. What began as busy work schedules, errands, raising children, work clothes, business meetings, and overtime becomes added time together. Without a plan for continued growth in the marriage relationship the potential for the couple to become distant in passion and communication multiplies. Pursuing one another in heart, soul, mind, and strength are important to the couple engaging in romance, conversation, and activities should be a part of every retirement conversation.

Conversation with the Bride and Groom

How does the couple plan to continue investing their heart, soul, mind, and strength in the future regarding the retirement years? Retirement may not be on the near horizon. Communicating desires for later years becomes a priority the closer the season comes. How has the couple begun to plan? (Home, finances, travel, relationship, retreats, community involvement, volunteering)

Time: Communicating today about the future. The retirement years redefine the time available. How much time has been dedicated to retirement planning? What plans have been made for the time the couple will spend together during retirement years?

Act: How will the couple continue to offer recognition or affirmation when advancements in career or vocation are no longer a part of their routine? How do they pursue one another in activities that have taken the place of their career?

Gift: Limited resources. Lean years. Fixed incomes. How is the couple creative in giving one another gifts of appreciation and affection? What small or inexpensive gifts have been favorites? What place do gifts serve in the couple's true personalities? (Are gifts paramount to their relationship)

Verbal: Retirement years multiplies time available for conversation. Having a reading plan for each offers subject matter. What conversations are anticipated? How are topics of conversation discovered? How creative is the couple in communication?

Touch: The time available for couples to linger for holding hands, touch, snuggles, or otherwise being together multiplies during retirement years. How does the couple plan to continue pursuing one another during retirement? What routines are in place that helps the couple plan for being alone during retirement? What changes in physical abilities or desire are concerns? How has each one begun to prepare for the future regarding touch?

Hobbies and Interests

Hobbies and interests occupy a couple's time not dedicated to work, family, volunteering, religious activities, and vacation. Although hobbies and interests may intersect those, hobbies and interests help the couple relax or enjoy recreation while doing something that engages their mind and body without a threat to career or jeopardizing their job. Some hobbies and interests are expensive and while others require little or no financial investment. Prior marriage, couples should weigh the cost of continuing hobbies or interests that drain funds from prioritized expenses.

Couples known for possessing a skillset that is valuable to others may want to consider coaching or mentoring others for a small fee that helps recoup expenses. The couple may choose to set aside a hobby or interest for a season until funds are readily available. Discussing the options prepares the couple to suspend an activity until later without causing undue resentment or frustration.

Conversation with Bride and Groom.

How will the couple invest their heart, soul, mind, and strength through engaging in one another's hobbies and interests as they grow together through the years?

Time: How often is the couple involved in a hobby? What plans have been made to postpone or give up a hobby for a season? What hobbies require time away from home or family? What priority has been compromised because of involvement in hobbies or interests?

Act: Including one another in Hobbies and Interests helps build unity in the marriage. Invite one another to join in creating memories. Encourage and challenge one another to refine skills. How often are each included in the other's hobbies or interests?

Gift: How are results of being involved in a hobby shared? What plans are there to share any profits from involvement? How often are objects of affection given that promote a hobby or interest or supply a need? Giving toward another's hobby shows sincerity and recognition of importance.

Verbal: If hobbies bring in extra income or benefits, how does the couple encourage one another to pursue or build skills? How often does the couple discuss benefits or liabilities of extra time and effort that could be invested in other areas of marriage?

Political views

The moral and faith values of the couple help establish or define the political views. Political views shared within the home become opportunities to discuss important issues facing the couple's home, faith, family, and community. Voting preferences, relaying important policy or candidate information, and discussing impacts of elections won or lost unite the couple in purpose and vision.

The purpose for discussing political views early in marriage is to build awareness of the volatile nature of political issues. Couples with similar political views stand better united in conversations outside of the home or with family members with opposing views. Being informed of policies, candidates, or balloted issues allows the couple to discuss topics within the context of their worldview and values.

Conversation with the Bride and Groom.

How does the couple reflect their heart, soul, mind, and strength as they engage in the political process? Politics and romance are opposite ends of the spectrum, yet both are important to the marriage relationship.

Time: When the moment comes, how much time is committed to discussing political climate and views?

How has the couple spent time in the past discussing political differences and similarities? What results are of concern?

Act/Gift: How does each recognize their differences in political views? How does the couple anticipate being active in the political process?

Verbal: Conversation allows each to affirm views, encourage debate, and challenge one another to conduct proper research to make informed decisions. How does the couple prompt one another to engage in meaningful political conversation? What conversations in the past have discouraged future conversation? What topics has the couple agreed to dismiss? What concerns are there for future disagreements?

Insurance

Preparing for the inevitable emergencies or family crisis is prudent. Insurance will not keep turbulent or tragic events from occurring, but it will at least give peace of mind knowing expenses are bearable. Insurance companies provide a wide range of protection from loss, damage, theft, or long-term health issues. Couples with basic policies for home, medical, life, and vehicle insurance are not doomsday preppers, but wise in gaining added protection and provision for their family.

Assigning the couple to have this discussion prior to a follow-up session allows the couple to investigate their current needs and contact a provider to fill in details or make recommendations.

Conversation with the Bride and Groom.

How does the couple invest their heart, soul, mind, and strength as they prepare for the inevitable inconveniences of difficult circumstances or crisis? (Protection, honor, responsibility, safety net) When did the couple last audit their insurance coverage? What updates will need to be made to existing policies? Who has them listed as beneficiaries to policies? What plans are offered by employers? How are bank accounts connected to policies? What other relatives are listed on the couple's policies?

Time: Insurance is a benefit recognized only when needed. Time dedicated to understanding policies and rules is important before signing to buy. How often does the couple set aside time to audit needs? How long are policies active? When are the renewal dates? (Time and dates for renewals should be posted in a prominent place to prevent lapses in coverage.)

Act/Gift: How has the couple benefited from insurance in the past? How does that past experience influence their decision currently? What is the current status of the couple's insurance audit? How can the couple use added coverage as a gift for the future or future generations?

Verbal: What concerns have been answered? What decisions must be made? How does discussing insurance benefit or hinder the couple's relationship or dreams for the future?

CHAPTER 5

Resources For Counselors

Resources abound for the minister or counselor investing in the lives of couples preparing for marriage. The statement of faith and practice of TwoTwentyfive affirms the primary source of wise counsel for marriage comes from the Bible. TwoTwentyfive recognizes there are a multitude of excellent theological and practical marriage resources available to ministers and counselors. Denominations, faith communities, associations, fellowships, and agencies both public and private offer counselors and couples a variety of resources already compatible with faith or belief traditions. Those who assist in preparing couples for marriage are encouraged to build their personal libraries with trusted resources easily navigated to benefit both counselor and client. Personal libraries accumulate choice resources from peers and counselors who know the local culture and are active in building relationships with others passionate about investing in the lives of the families they serve. Building strong communities with strong families requires ministers, counselors, attorneys, and social workers to take time nurturing strong marriages. Grow your resources and contact list. Know who you can refer to in confidence. If agency or personal budgets are restricted, use the resources at local libraries or peers. Borrowed books are preferred rather than debt. Ask about resources available in church libraries. Keep a list of desired resources available for times when books are on sale, or a family member asks about birthday or Christmas ideas! Below are recommended starting points.

- Alcorn, Randy, *The Treasure Principle: Unlocking the Secret of Joyful Giving*. Colorado Springs, CO: Multnomah Books, 2001.
- Baucham, Voddie, *Family Shepherds: Calling and Equipping Men to Lead Their Homes*. Wheaton, IL: Crossway, 2011.
- Bolton, Robert, *People Skills: How to Assert Yourself, Listen to Others, and Resolve Conflicts*. New York, NY: Simon & Schuster, 1979.
- Carroll, Elizabeth and Jim, *Marriage Boot Camp: Defeat the Top Ten Marriage Killers and*

Build a Rock-Solid Relationship. New York: New American Library, 2016.

- Chapman, Gary, *Now You're Speaking My Love Language: Honest Communication and Deeper Intimacy for a Stronger Marriage*. Nashville: B&H Publishing Group, 2007.

- Christensen, James L, *The Minister's Marriage Handbook*. Old Tappan: Fleming H.

- Revell Company, 1985.

- Cloud, Henry, and John Townsend, *Boundaries in Marriage*. Grand Rapids: Zondervan, 1999.

- Cloud, Henry, and John Townsend, *How to Have That Difficult Conversation: Gaining the Skills for Honest and Meaningful Communication*. Grand Rapids: Zondervan, 2003.

- Crosson, Russ, *Your Life Well Spent: The Eternal Rewards of Investing Yourself and Your Money in Your Family*. Eugene: Harvest House Publishers, 1994.

- Debinski, Craig and Pamela, *Excellent Marriage: A Training Manual to Equip You in Discovering God's Grand Design*. San Francisco: Timeless Texts, open source, 2001.

- Delffs, Dudley, *Mastering Money*. Colorado Springs: NavPress, 1998.

- Farrell, Bill and Pam, *The Before-You-Marry Book of Question*. Eugene: Harvest House, 2013.

- Florida Bar, *Family Law Handbook*. Tallahassee: The Florida Bar, Family Law Section, 2020.

- Focus on the Family. https://focusonthefamily.com/marriage/.

- Godek, Gregory, *1001 Ways To Be Romantic: A Handbook for Men-A Godsend for Women*. New York: Penguin Group, 2010.

- Gottman, John M., *The Seven Principles for Making Marriage Work*. New York: Three Rivers Press, 1999.

- Green, Rob, *Tying the Knot: A Premarital Guide to a Strong and Lasting Marriage* Greensboro: New Growth Press, 2016.

- Harley, Willard F., *His Needs Her Needs: Building an Affair-Proof Marriage*. Grand Rapids: Revell, 2009.

- Harley, Willard F., *Love Busters: Protect Your Marriage by Replacing Love-Busting Patterns with Love-Building Habits*. Grand Rapids: Revel, 2016.

- Henry, Jim, *The Pastor's Wedding Manual*. Nashville: Broadman Press, 1985.

- Hobbs, J. R., *The Pastor's Manual*. Nashville: Broadman Press, 1962.

- Leman, Dr. Kevin, *Becoming a Couple of Promise*. Colorado Springs: NavPress, 1999.

- McKay, Matthew, Martha Davis, and Patrick Fanning, *Messages: The Communication Skills Book*. Oakland: New Harbinger Publications, 1983.

- Smalley, Gary, *I Promise: How 5 Commitments Determine the Destiny of Your Marriage*. Nashville: Thomas Nelson, 2006.

- Smalley, Dr. Greg and Erin. *Crazy Little Thing Called Marriage: 12 Secrets for a Lifelong Romance*. Carol Stream: Tyndale House Publishers, 2015.

- Statutes & Constitution: View Statutes: Online Sunshine (state.fl.us), Title XLIII Chapter 741, Marriage; Domestic Violence. www.state.fl.us. statues/index.

- SYMBIS. https://www.symbis.com/couples/.

- Tripp, Paul David, *What Did You Expect? Redeeming the Realities of Marriage*. Wheaton: Crossway, 2010.

- Young, Ed, *Romancing the Home: How to Have a Marriage that Sizzles*. Nashville: Broadman & Holman Publishers, 1994.

CHAPTER 6

Resources for Couples

Homes need good books that challenge couples and families to be their best. The number of recommendable books increase every year. Classic books from known authors or organizations such as Focus on the Family, Gary Chapman, Kevin Leman, and Greg Smalley are filled with timeless principles. Newer authors continue to update principles that apply to current culture and media availability. Counselors should have a short list of "best books" to recommend to couples who are a part of faith communities or express similar faith or belief values. Below are several recommendations that are available in print or digital media and easily read and passed along to other couples.

- Baucham, Voddie, *Family Shepherds: Calling and Equipping Men to Lead Their Homes*. Wheaton, IL: Crossway, 2011.

- Carroll, Elizabeth and Jim, *Marriage Boot Camp: Defeat the Top Ten Marriage Killers and Build a Rock-Solid Relationship*. New York: New American Library, 2016.

- Chapman, Gary, *Now You're Speaking My Love Language: Honest Communication and Deeper Intimacy for a Stronger Marriage*. Nashville: B&H Publishing Group, 2007.

- Crosson, Russ, *Your Life Well Spent: The Eternal Rewards of Investing Yourself and Your Money in Your Family*. Eugene: Harvest House Publishers, 1994.

- Delffs, Dudley, *Mastering Money*. Colorado Springs: NavPress, 1998.

- Farrell, Bill and Pam, *The Before-You-Marry Book of Question*. Eugene: Harvest House, 2013.

- Florida Bar, *Family Law Handbook*. Tallahassee: The Florida Bar, Family Law Section, 2020.

- Focus on the Family. https://focusonthefamily.com/marriage/.

- Harley, Willard F., *His Needs Her Needs: Building an Affair-Proof Marriage*. Grand Rapids: Revell, 2009.

- Harley, Willard F., *Love Busters: Protect Your Marriage by Replacing Love-Busting Patterns with Love-Building Habits*. Grand Rapids: Revel, 2016.

- Godek, Gregory, *1001 Ways To Be Romantic: A Handbook for Men-A Godsend for Women*. New York: Penguin Group, 2010.
- Leman, Dr. Kevin, *Becoming a Couple of Promise*. Colorado Springs: NavPress, 1999.
- Smalley, Gary, *I Promise: How 5 Commitments Determine the Destiny of Your Marriage*. Nashville: Thomas Nelson, 2006.
- Smalley, Dr. Greg and Erin. *Crazy Little Thing Called Marriage: 12 Secrets for a Lifelong Romance*. Carol Stream: Tyndale House Publishers, 2015.
- Statutes & Constitution: View Statutes: Online Sunshine (state.fl.us), Title XLIII Chapter 741, Marriage; Domestic Violence. www.state.fl.us. statues/index.
- SYMBIS. https://www.symbis.com/couples/.
- Tripp, Paul David, *What Did You Expect? Redeeming the Realities of Marriage*. Wheaton: Crossway, 2010.
- Young, Ed, *Romancing the Home: How to Have a Marriage that Sizzles*. Nashville:
- Broadman & Holman Publishers, 1994.

WEDDING INFORMATION

BRIDE

Name: _____

Address: _____

Phone: _____

Email: _____

Occupation: _____

Parents: _____

Faith Background: _____

_____

How would you classify the parent's attitude toward the marriage?

_____

Is there any opposition to the marriage from family?

_____

What preparations have you made for marriage? (Consultation with doctor, minister, reading, prayer)

_____

Are you having a physical before the wedding?

_____

When was your last physical?

_____

GROOM

Name: _____

Address: _____

Phone: _____

Email: _____

Occupation: _____

Parents: _____

Faith Background: _____

_____

How would you classify the parent's attitude toward the marriage?

_____

Is there any opposition to the marriage from family?

_____

What preparations have you made for marriage? (Consultation with doctor, minister, reading, prayer)

_____

Are you having a physical before the wedding?

_____

When was your last physical?

_____

Dates for Marriage Counseling:

_____

_____

_____

Wedding Party:

Best Man: _____

Maid of Honor: _____

Groomsmen/Attendants: _____

_____

_____

_____

_____

_____

_____

Ceremony Details:

Place/venue? _____

Date of rehearsal? _____

Date of wedding? _____

Wedding Officiant/s: _____

_____

Who will have the license? _____

NOTES: _____

_____

_____

_____

PREMARITAL COUNSELING QUICK REFERENCE

Commitment

How does the couple invest their heart, soul, mind, and strength in their commitment to one another? How do they *currently* express to one another their commitment to their marriage with each love language? (Time, Act, Gift, Verbal, Touch)

Communication

How does the couple invest their heart, soul, mind, and strength in honest communication with one another? How do they *currently* communicate to one another in each love language? (Time, Act, Gift, Verbal, Touch)

Intimacy

How does the couple invest their heart, soul, mind, and strength within the context of intimacy? How do they *currently* express intimacy in each love language? (Time, Act, Gift, Verbal, Touch) [faith and practice]

Finances

How does the couple invest their heart, soul, mind, and strength while cooperating in the goal of financial security? How do they *currently* define financial success and stewardship?

Faith

How does the couple invest their heart, soul, mind, and strength in their spiritual growth and faith journey together? (Being one in heart, soul, mind, and strength) How familiar are they with each other's spiritual journey? How do they *currently* share their faith in each love language? (Time, Act, Gift, Verbal, Touch)

Family

How does the couple invest their heart, soul, mind, and strength as they become not only their own family but a part one another's extended family? (Emotional connections, appreciation, understanding, position)

Conflict Resolution

How does the couple invest their heart, soul, mind, and strength in navigating through conflicts? How does the couple currently resolve disagreements or conflict?

Career

How does the couple invest their heart, soul, mind, and strength in supporting and encouraging one another's careers? How will the couple manage future career or position advancements?

Friends

How does the couple invest their heart, soul, mind, and strength in one another as they appreciate the other's friendship relationships? How do they protect their marriage relationship?

Vacation time

How does the couple invest their heart, soul, mind, and strength as they plan and participate in recreational activities? How does the couple focus on one another and build a stronger bond between husband and wife, parent and child, or siblings?

Holidays/Travel

How does the couple invest their heart, soul, mind, and strength in their marriage while honoring family or extended family? What past experiences remain a concern or prompt a new tradition?

Community Involvement

How does the couple engage their heart, soul, mind, and strength as a couple as they participate and become known in their community? How is the couple currently known in their community? How does the couple want to be known?

Education/Professional Training

How does the couple invest their heart, soul, mind, and strength in one another and their marriage as they pursue further education or professional training? How does the training or education benefit the marriage and future plans?

Social Views

How does the couple share their heart, soul, mind, and strength while participating in social action or expressing social views publicly? What major differences and concerns have been discussed or agreed upon?

Personal Health (Staying Healthy)

How does the couple continue to engage their heart, soul, mind, and strength through a healthy lifestyle, setting a precedent for continued growth? (Whole-being health: heart, soul, mind, body)

What common activities enlighten their hearts and draw them closer?

Will/s

How does the couple plan to invest their heart, soul, mind, and strength in the future regarding a will that benefits one another or family? Does each have a will? Have they discussed with one another or family about writing a will?

Retirement plans

How does the couple plan to continue investing their heart, soul, mind, and strength in the future regarding the retirement years? How has the couple begun to plan? (Home, finances, travel, relationship, retreats, community involvement, volunteering)

Hobbies and Interests

How does the couple invest their heart, soul, mind, and strength through engaging in one another's hobbies and interests as they grow together through the years? What interests and hobbies does the couple share/plan to share?

Political views

How does the couple reflect their heart, soul, mind, and strength as they engage in the political process? How has the couple agreed to discuss differing views and pursue compromise when needed?

Insurance

How does the couple invest their heart, soul, mind, and strength as they prepare for the inevitable inconveniences of difficult circumstances or crises? (Protection, honor, responsibility, safety net) When did the couple last audit or update their insurance coverage?